Summary of William W. Li, MD's *Eat To Beat Disease: The New Science of How Your Body Can Heal Itself* Overview & Analysis by Summary Genie

Note to readers:

This is an unofficial summary & analysis of William W. Li, MD's *Eat To Beat Disease: The New Science of How Your Body Can Heal Itself* designed to enrich your reading experience. Please buy the original book through Amazon.

Disclaimer: All Rights Reserved. No part of this publication may be reproduced or retransmitted, electronic or mechanical, without the written permission of the publisher; with the exception of brief quotes used in connection in reviews written for inclusion in a magazine or newspaper. This book is licensed for your personal enjoyment only. This book may not be re-sold or given away to other people. If you would like to share this book with another person, please purchase an additional copy for each recipient. If you're reading this book and did not purchase it, or it was not purchased for your use only, then please purchase your own copy.

Product names, logos, brands, and other trademarks featured or referred to within this publication are the property of their respective trademark holders. These trademark holders are not affiliated with us and they do not sponsor or endorse our publications. This book is unofficial and unauthorized. It is not authorized, approved, licensed, or endorsed by the aforementioned interests or any of their licensees.

The information in this book has been provided for educational and entertainment purposes only.

The information contained in this book has been compiled from sources deemed reliable and it is accurate to the best of the Author's knowledge; however, the Author cannot guarantee its accuracy and validity and cannot be held liable for any errors or omissions. Upon using the information contained in this book, you agree to hold harmless the author from and against any damages, costs, and expenses, including any legal fees, potentially resulting from the application of any of the information provided by this guide. The disclaimer applies to any damages or injury caused by the use and application, whether directly or indirectly, of any advice or information presented, whether for breach of contract, tort, neglect, personal injury, criminal intent, or under any other cause of action. You agree to accept all risks of using the information presented inside this book.

The fact that an individual or organization is referred to in this document as a citation or source of information does not imply that the author or publisher endorses the information that the individual or organization provided. This is an unofficial summary & analytical review and has not been approved by the original author of the book.

© 2019 Summary Genie

Your Free Gift!

As a way to say, "**Thank You!**" for being a fan of our summaries, we've included a **Free Gift** for you-a powerful brain program that helps **Increase Your IQ, Memory and Focus** *Fast!*

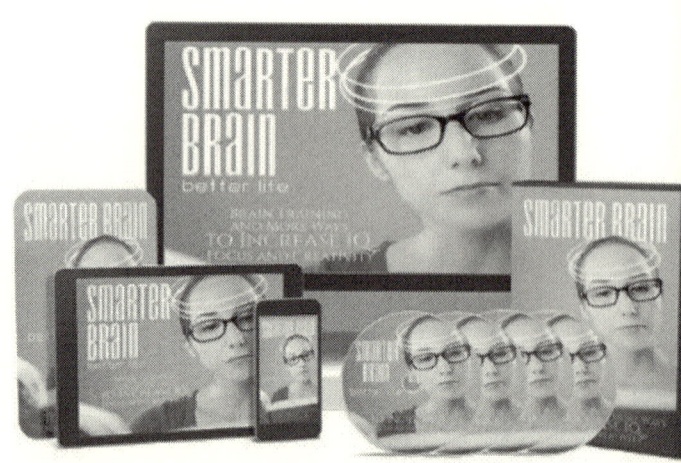

To receive your free gift, please visit:
https://summarygenie.aweb.page/freegift

Thank you once again!

The Summary Genie Team

Table of Contents

Summary of Eat To Beat Disease by William W. Li, MD

Chapter by Chapter Analysis

Part I: Hardwired for Health: Our Body's Natural Defense Systems

- Chapter 1: Angiogenesis
- Chapter 2: Regeneration
- Chapter 3: Microbiome
- Chapter 4: DNA Protection
- Chapter 5: Immunity

Part II: Eat to Beat Disease: The Evidence for Food as Medicine

- Chapter 6: Starve Your Disease, Feed Your Health
- Chapter 7: (Re)generate Your Health
- Chapter 8: Feed Your Inner Ecosystem
- Chapter 9: Direct Your Genetic Fate
- Chapter 10: Activate Your Immune Command Center

Part Three, Plan, Choose and Act: Putting Food To Work

- Chapter 11: The 5x5x5 Framework: Eating to Beat Disease
- Chapter 12: Rethinking the Kitchen
- Chapter 13: Exceptional Foods
- Chapter 14: Sample Meal Guide and Recipes
- Chapter 15: Food Doses

Background information about Eat To Beat Disease

Background information about William W. Li, MD

Summary of *Eat To Beat Disease* by William W. Li, MD

Eat To Beat Disease is the non-fiction best-seller by William W. Li, a medical doctor and the leader of the Angiogenesis Foundation. Dr. Li believes that in today's world, rates of new disease are needlessly skyrocketing, specifically in terms of dangerous noncommunicable diseases such as cancer, diabetes and obesity.

New drug treatments can help, but they are not the only answer; ideally, for Dr. Li we would prevent disease rather than need to cure it. Thus, he has turned to diet to search for the answer for how to live longer, healthier lives – at a lower cost than medical treatment would require.

Dr. Li's plan is based on his belief that the body has five defense systems that form key pillars of health, each of which is influence by what we eat. The five systems – each of which are discussed in the first five chapters – are angiogenesis (the process by which our blood vessels are formed), regeneration (how our body regenerates itself on a daily basis), microbiome (the bacteria that live in our bodies and boost immunity), DNA protection (the way our DNA can fix itself to fight disease), and immunity (the way we react to external pathogens).

In this book, which is not a "diet" book geared toward losing weight or dealing with some dietary intolerance, Dr. Li gives readers the tools to make better decisions about what they eat every day, so they can live longer and in better condition.

Eat To Beat Disease is divided into three parts.

Part I: Hardwired for Health: Our Body's Natural Defense Systems, tells the story of health defense systems and how we can put them to work for our health. It has five chapters. Chapter 1: Angiogenesis, Chapter 2: Regeneration, Chapter 3: Microbiome, Chapter 4: DNA Protection, Chapter 5: Immunity.

Part II: Eat to Beat Disease: The Evidence for Food as Medicine, goes over the foods that activate our health defense systems. It also has five chapters: Chapter 6: Starve Your Disease, Feed Your Health, Chapter 7: (Re)generate Your Health, Chapter 8: Feed Your Inner Ecosystem, Chapter 9: Direct Your Genetic Fate, Chapter 10: Activate Your Immune Command Center.

Part Three: Plan, Choose and Act: Putting Food To Work, offers a simple way to start introducing these foods into your diet, along with a flexible tool to make sure you are choosing from the ideal food groups. It also has five chapters: chapter 11, the 5x5x5 Framework: Eating to Beat Disease, Chapter 12: Rethinking the Kitchen, Chapter 13: Exceptional Foods, Chapter 14: Sample Meal Guide and Recipes, Chapter 15: Food Doses.

Chapter by Chapter Analysis

Part I: Hardwired for Health: Our Body's Natural Defense Systems

Chapter 1: Angiogenesis

Believe it or not, every human alive has cancer growing in their body – microscopic tumors that for most people will never become dangerous. Our bodies use their natural defenses to cut off blood supply to these would-be tumors, ensuring that they do us no harm. Dr. Li believes there are more than one hundred foods that help our bodies achieve these goals, including soy, tomatoes, black raspberries and pomegranate, as well as licorice, beer and cheese.

The process our bodies use to stop cancer before it starts is called angiogenesis, the way in which our bodies grow and maintain blood vessels. We need blood vessels to deliver oxygen and nutrients all through our bodies, but they can also end up inadvertently nourishing cancer cells. When our angiogenesis system is healthy, it regulates the growth of these blood cells and makes sure tumors do not use them to take over an organ.

Angiogenesis is so essential to human life that it starts in a woman's body even before conception. We can witness angiogenesis when we cut ourselves and the wound starts to show changes in the first few moments, as the blood coagulates and a scab forms. That red patch is the sign of thousands of new blood vessels growing to restore the injured tissue.

Our bodies regulate angiogenesis on the basis of what we need – too much, and we can get cancer or loss of vision or even Alzheimer's'; too little and we can experience tissue loss or diabetes. Luckily food can help us maintain or restore this balance.

Chapter 2: Regeneration

Stem cells are the body's secret weapon in maintaining and growing our organs. Without stem cells, our bodies could not survive a week. The older we are, the slower our organs regenerate itself, making a healthy diet all the more important with age. Stem cells are what our body calls on in the event of injury, functioning like a guided missile that hones in on a target.

They are non-specialized cells, so they can go wherever they are needed a transform themselves based on whatever it is they need to do in terms of repairing the injured tissue.

Stem cells can get damaged by many factors, including cigarette smoke and second hand smoke, as well as air pollution, and heavy drinking. Having high cholesterol can impair stem cell function, as can chronic diseases like diabetes. The good news is that by taking steps to boost our stem cells through diet, we can make a positive impact on our health.

Chapter 3: Microbiome

Thanks to advances in science, we can now say that humans are not actually humans, we are "holobionts." This fantastical sounding word simply means that our body is not just a single entity but is an entire ecosystem that includes 39 trillion bacteria, most of which are good, that comprise around three pounds of our body weight.

Doctors once thought all bacteria had to be expunged, but no we know that they are necessary for our survival, regulating our endocrine or hormonal systems, and helping to reduce stress and anxiety. These bacteria also get involved in angiogenesis, stem cells and immunity. Some scientists believe they influence social behavior.

Living in symbiosis with our microbiome is crucial to good health, and food is a huge factor in keeping our microbiome happy. Our bacteria consume what we consume, and the result of their metabolic activity has a profound effect on our health. Specifically, we need to strive for a diverse microbiome, which gives us more strength to fight a range of conditions.

We introduce new bacteria into our microbiome constantly, for example through kissing other people. Food is one of the most common points of entry for these bacteria, and the foods that have an influence on the microbiome are called probiotics (foods that contain living bacteria like yogurt) or prebiotics (nondigestible foods that the bacteria consume, including dietary fibers).

Eating a natural diet with lots of diversity is the best way to influence or microbiome. Processed foods, instead, limit our bodies' ability to heal itself through the microbiome and can have harmful consequences for years.

Chapter 4: DNA Protection

Our DNA is a double helix structure that contains our personal genetic blueprint. DNA is not just important, it is also fragile, and it can be attacked by any number of factors that threaten its ability to direct the workings of our bodies.

Air pollution, cigarette smoke and UV rays can harm DNA, as can toxic chemicals in our environment; radon, a chemical that emerges from the ground can be very damaging to DNA. And of course, food has a huge impact on the way that DNA reproduces itself.

When DNA makes a mistake in how it produces copies, the resulting mutations can be devastating to our health. Therefore, DNA tries to protect itself, including with cellular "repair crews" (enzymes) that edit out the mistaken instructions.

Telomeres are another protective factor, acting like aglets (the caps that cover the tips of shoelaces) at the end of each chromosome, working to protect your DNA from wear and tear that happens as a normal part of the aging process. Diet, sleep and exercise can all help protect these important structures.

Another way DNA protects itself is through epigenetic change, which is how DNA changes after birth, as certain genes get turned on or off based on the environmental influence. Our diet can impact these epigenetic changes, for better or for worse.

Chapter 5: Immunity

Our immune system can help protect us against everything from the common cold to cancer, and our diet has a huge influence on our immune system. When the immune system is weakened, that is when the tiny cancer cells in our body can make huge inroads against us.

Our immune system is strong because it is structured like a military with different branches that are each specialized against a different kind of intruder. There are four centers of immunity: the bone marrow (spongey material in the hollow areas of bone), the thymus (an organ located behind the breastbone), the spleen (located behind the stomach on the left, it stores and filters blood) and lymph nodes (located throughout the body in the neck, armpits and groin), and the gut (all of which is an immune organ).

The soldiers of immunity are white blood cells or leukocytes, divided into dive different kinds, each of which specialize in a different kind of defense. Then, two different kind of immune systems are poised and ready to respond, one fast and one slow – an allergic reaction, for example, is dealt with quickly by the innate system. It is more simplistic and responds by causing an inflammation.

The more sophisticated immune system – the adaptive immune system – is also slower, and can take a week to kick into gear. It can attack invading cells or use antibodies, but since these take seven to ten days to be produced, this immune system has a slow response time. Luckily these cells also have a long memory, so if you get attacked by the same thing again, they are ready to respond much quicker.

Are you enjoying the book so far?

If so, please help us reach more readers by taking
30 seconds to write
just a few words on Amazon

**Thank you very much!
Now, let's continue…**

Part II: Eat to Beat Disease: The Evidence for Food as Medicine

Chapter 6: Starve Your Disease, Feed Your Health

This chapter focuses on foods that can help you keep your angiogenesis defenses in balance to avoid contracting a range of feared diseases, foremost amongst them cancer. It is important to distinguish between diseases caused by too much angiogenesis and too little.

In the first group, we have heart disease and cancer. To avoid these diseases, focus on antiangiogenic foods. In the second group, risk of stroke can be caused by too little angiogenesis. To avoid these diseases, focus on angiogenetic foods.

Antiangiogenic foods

- **Soy**

Soy is a powerful antiangiogenic, thought to be responsible for positive health outcomes in Japan. Because it is high in isoflavones, an antiangiogenic molecule, soy products such as tofu, miso and tempeh can all be helpful. Fermented soy products in particular are high in isoflavones. Try for ten grams of soy protein per day, chosen from soybeans, soymilk or other traditional soy products.

- **Tomato**

This fruit contains lycopene, which has been proven to block angiogenesis. Make sure to eat the skin, as it has the highest concentration. Cooking tomatoes with the skin is also a great way to get the most out of the tomato. Using olive oil helps increase the amount of lycopene absorbed by your body.

- **Antiangiogenic vegetables**

The cruciferous family is highly potent in stopping angiogenesis. This includes broccoli, kale cauliflower and brussels sprouts.

- **Antiangiogenic fruits**

Stone fruits are great for stopping angiogenesis. Try plums in particular, as well as apricots. Fresh fruits are better than dry. Apples are also a good fruit to choose, but go for Granny Smith, Red Delicious and the Reinette. Berries are also good for boosting your body's defenses, the black raspberry in particular. (Try strawberries too.)

- **Seafood**

Seafood is an important component of a healthy diet, thanks to their omega-3s, as well as three other forms of fat including EPA and DHA. Fatty fish should be a necessary part of a healthy diet; if you don't live near the coast, by fish that is flash frozen at sea, which captures the omega-3s. The best fishes to choose include: hake, sea cucumber, manila clam, big eye tuna, yellowtail, sea bass, bluefin tuna, cockles, bottarga, caviar and fish roe. Tilapia should be avoided as it is low in omega-3s.

- **Chicken Thigh**

Although people tend to prefer the breast because it is low fat, dark meat has a lot of great vitamins, including K2, which has antiangiogenic properties. If you trim the fat off of chicken thighs, it is actually healthier than the breast.

- **Air-cured ham: what to do?**

Processed meat is listed by the World Health Organization as a carcinogen, but air-cured ham from Spain and Italy are somewhat of an exception. Because these pigs are fed the whey of parmigiano Reggiano cheese as babies, they taste great. They also are fed chestnuts or acorns which are high in omega-3s. This means that air-cured ham is a great source of omega-3s as well, which is preserved during their air curing process. However, these foods are extremely high in fat, so do not consider them a health food. Think about it as a luxury food to be used sparingly, not a main meal.

- **Beverages**

Tea is a great anti-angiogenetic food, particularly Chinese jasmine tea. Herbal chamomile tea can also have a positive effect.

- **Red wine**

The best wines to drink are Cabernet Sauvignon, Cabernet Franc and Petit Verdot – in moderation.

- **Beer**

Beer hops are powerfully antiangiogenic, and can be helpful in warding off cancer and helping improve the cardiovascular system, again in moderation.

- **Cheese**

Not typically associated with good health, cheese also contains vitamin K2 thanks to the bacterial starters used in cheese making. Because of the high amounts of saturated fat, cholesterol and high sodium, it is also important to be moderate with cheese; but we should not rule it out altogether as some popular diets propose.

- **Other Antiangiogenetic Foods**

  Olive oil, tree nuts and beans, dark chocolate, spices and herbs.

- **Angiogenetic Foods**

Grains and seeds, foods with ursolic acid (fruit skins, ginseng, rosemary and peppermint), foods rich in quercetin (capers, onions, red-leaf lettuce, hot green chili peppers, cranberries, black plums and apples).

Chapter 7: (Re)generate Your Health

This chapter discusses foods that harness the body's regenerative power, helping stem cells mobilize themselves to counteract and prevent the organ damage that comes with aging. These diseases include Parkinson's and Alzheimer's, as well as cardiovascular diseases, diabetes and osteoporosis.

- Fish oil is high in protective omega-3s, as are hake, tuna, yellowtail and shellfish.

Squid Ink, which comes from cuttlefish, is also known to help protect stem cells.

Whole wheat contains polyphenols and fiber, which helps protect against cardiovascular disease and diabetes. Rice bran is similarly protective, but make sure to buy it from California, India or Pakistan to avoid the crops that have higher arsenic levels.

- Green beans, eaten fresh or dried, can help our stem cells' regenerative properties.

Turmeric is a powerful root that is anti-inflammatory, antioxidant, antiangiogenic and pro-regenerative.

- Foods and drinks high in resveratrol: grapes, red wine and grape juice; blueberries, cranberries, peanuts and pistachios are also good choices. However, these foods have relatively low quantities of resveratrol, so a supplement may be a better choice.

- Foods high in zeaxanthin: corn, saffron and green leafy vegetables, as well as goji berries, have great benefits for eye health.

- Foods high in chlorogenic acid: coffee, black tea, blueberries, peaches, fresh and dried plums, eggplants and bamboo shoots, have powerful anti-inflammatory benefits.

- Black raspberries (consumed in a powder) are a potent source of helpful bioactives and, therefore, helpful to increase the circulation of stem cells.

- Chinese celery can be helpful in post-stroke recovery because of the increase in circulation of stem cells it promotes

- Mangoes contain numerous bioactives, one of which has antitumor, antidiabetic and pro-regenerative properties.

- Suggested beverages include red wine (moderate consumption), beer, green tea, and black tea

- Suggested dietary patterns to help stem cells: The Mediterranean diet, caloric restriction and fasting. The ketogenic diet – a very high fat, very low carb diet – can also be beneficial, because it makes the body feel like it is fasting, keeping glucose levels low and making it hard for tumors to keep growing.

- Dietary patterns to avoid in order to protect stem cells: diets high in saturated fats, hyperglycemic (very high sugar) foods, and high salt diets.

- Foods that kill cancer stem cells: Green tea, purple potatoes, walnuts, and extra virgin olive oil, as well as soy, celery, oregano, thyme, capers, apples and peppers. Studies suggest possible benefits from coffee, carrots and stone fruit, as well as red wine, grapes, peanuts, pistachios, dark chocolate and cranberries, chestnuts, blackberries and pomegranates.

Chapter 8: Feed Your Inner Ecosystem

Many diseases can spring up when the microbiome is out of whack. Gastrointestinal cancers are more common in people with disturbed microbiomes, as are inflammatory bowel diseases, and even some cardiovascular disease, Parkinson's and Alzheimer's. Chances of asthma are also increased.

Food is an easy way to support our microbiome, by eating foods with healthy bacteria (live cultures) such as sauerkraut, kimchi (the Korean fermented vegetables), and Pao Cai (Chinese fermented cabbage).

Cheese, including Parmiggiano-Reggiano (Italian), camembert and gouda are excellent ways to help our microbiome, as is yogurt. Sourdough bread, made with a live starter, is known to improve immunity and suppress tumor growth.

Other overall guidelines to support the microbiome include: eat plant based whole foods with lots of dietary fiber; eat less animal protein; and eat more fresh, whole foods and reduce processed foods.

In addition, make sure to eat foods that have a positive effect on the microbiome, including pumpernickel bread, kiwi, cruciferous vegetables, bamboo shoots, dark chocolate, walnuts, beans, mushrooms. Beverages such as fruit juices (pomegranate, cranberry and concord grape), red wine and teas are also beneficial.

Avoid artificial sweeteners including saccharine, aspartame, sucralose, acesulfame and neotame.

Be extra attentive to your microbiome if you ever have to take antibiotics, which kill good and bad bacteria.

Chapter 9: Direct Your Genetic Fate

Many diseases are caused by DNA damage, foremost among them skin cancer, as well as lung, bladder, esophagus, stomach and colon cancer.

DNA repair can be influenced by foods such as: berry juices, kiwi, carrots, broccoli, watermelon, tomato, guava, pink grapefruit, seafood, and pacific oysters.

Some foods are known to activate positive factors in your DNA or shut off negative ones, including: soy, cruciferous veggies, coffee, tea, turmeric, and herbs.

Other foods protect fragile telomeres including: coffee, tea, nuts and seeds, the Mediterranean and Asian diets.

Foods to avoid include: fatty foods, processed meats, and sugar-sweetened beverages

Chapter 10: Activate Your Immune Command Center

Immune conditions can open our body up to a host of problems, including cancer; an overactive immune system can lead to autoimmune diseases, including lupus, diabetes and MS.

To boost immune function, try mushrooms, aged garlic, broccoli sprouts, extra virgin olive oil, chestnuts, blackberries, black raspberries, walnuts and pomegranate. Fruit juices such as cranberry and concord grape juice are also recommended. Blueberries are another powerful immune booster, as are Chile Peppers, Pacific oysters, and Licorice root.

To calm inflammation and autoimmunity in the case of an overactive immune system, increase your intake of Vitamin C, Green Tea, or try a Raw vegan living diet (eating foods in their natural and unprocessed state), high vegetable low protein diet, and an autoimmune protocol diet (similar to the Paleo diet).

Are you enjoying the book so far?

If so, please help us reach more readers by taking
30 seconds to write
just a few words on Amazon

**Thank you very much!
Now, let's continue...**

Part III, Plan, Choose and Act: Putting Food To Work

Chapter 11: The 5x5x5 Framework: Eating to Beat Disease

This framework is not a weight-loss diet and is adaptable to whatever current diet you are following. Using the foods listed in Part II, create a list of preferred foods. Every day, pick five foods and make sure to eat all five in one day, whether in the same or different meals.

Pick the foods you enjoy eating, and incorporate them in a way that is sustainable. Don't worry if you miss a day, just keep on going. If a food gets boring to you, pick a different one instead. Remember, if you are battling a serious disease, discuss your diet with your doctor.

Chapter 12: Rethinking the Kitchen

Tools for a healthier relationship to food include:

Various knives for chopping and paring, metal tongs, a colander, high-quality pans, stockpot, cast-iron Dutch oven, glass or ceramic baking dishes, baking sheets, bamboo steamer, wok, rice cooker, food mill, toaster oven, wooden cutting board, vegetable peeler, can opener, metal whisk, microplane grater, pepper mill, wooden spoons, stainless ladle, blender, glass liquid measuring cup, stainless steel dry measuring cups, metal measuring spoons, coffee mills (for coffee and spices), French press coffeemaker, automatic hot water dispenser, wine opener or corkscrew, glass food storage containers.

Foods to keep n your pantry include:

Extra virgin olive oil and real vinegars, dried spices, black pepper, dried beans, rice, flour, pasta, coffee, tea, nuts, dried fruits and mushrooms, tinned seafood, whole grains, seeds and capers. Include sauces such as: sriracha, chili paste, canned tomatoes, tomato paste, anchovy paste, miso paste, oyster sauce, and soy. Good sweeteners include: honey, maple syrup and maple sugar.

Good cooking techniques include: steaming, blanching, stir-frying, sautéing, poaching, simmering, braising, slow cooking pressure cooking, a la plancha (on the griddle), grilling, roasting, baking, marinating, pickling.

More tips: eat the entire vegetable, including skins, the greens on the tops of carrots, the broccoli and mushroom stems, etc; avoid deep frying and do not reuse oils; reheat food on stovetop or in oven, not in the microwave.

Chapter 13: Exceptional Foods

Unusual foods that the author highly recommends include: squash blossoms, persimmons, fresh wasabi, bitter melon, fiddleheads, truffles, bottarga (salty dried fish roe), squid ink, and razor clams.

The author also includes the foods he considers to be "Grand Slammers," the select list of the absolute best foods to choose on a daily basis.

- Fruits: apricots, blueberries, cherries, kiwi, lychee, mangoes, nectarines, peaches and plums

- Vegetables: bamboo shoots, carrots, eggplant, fiddleheads and kale

- Beverages: black tea, chamomile tea, coffee and green tea

- Nuts/seeds: flax, pumpkin, sesame, sunflower and walnuts

- Seafood: squid ink

- Oil: extra virgin

- Sweets: dark chocolate

Chapter 14: Sample Meal Guide and Recipes

This chapter contains a suggested list of daily foods to eat to meet the 5x5x5 framework, as well as possible recipes to try.

Chapter 15: Food Doses

Dr. Li believes that foods, like medicines, have proper doses, that can be linked to a specific health outcome. A list of important food doses and their benefits includes:

- Apples, 1-2 per day, to prevent bladder and colorectal cancer

- Apricots, 2 per day, to prevent esophageal and head/neck cancer

- Bamboo shoots, 1/3 cup per day, to prevent metabolic syndrome

- Beer, 1 per day, to prevent colorectal cancer and coronary artery disease; five per week to prevent kidney cancer; 1-2 per day to prevent dementia

- Black raspberries: 2 cups per day for Barrett's esophagus, 7 cups per day for Bladder cancer, 4 berries per day for cardiovascular disease.

- Black tea: 2 cups per day for hypertension

- Blackberries: 5 ½ cups per day for bladder cancer

- Blueberries, 1 cup per week for breast cancer

- Bluefish, 1+ servings per week for macular degeneration, 3.5 oz. per day for colorectal cancer

- Broccoli: 1-2 cups per week for breast and esophageal cancer, 2 cups per day for lupus

- Cashews: 26 nuts per day for colorectal cancer

- Cherries: 2 fruits to prevent esophageal and head/neck cancer

- Chestnuts: 1.7 oz. per day to prevent bladder cancer

- Coffee: 2+ cups per day, to prevent myocardial infarction

- Dark chocolate: 375 milligrams flavonoids per day to prevent coronary artery disease

- Dark meat chicken: 1 drumstick/thigh per day to prevent colorectal cancer

- Edam cheese: 2 slices per day to prevent colorectal cancer

- Edamame: 1.2 cups per day to prevent breast cancer

- Fermented kimchi: 1.2 cups per day to prevent obesity

- Fish: 3 oz. per day to prevent colorectal and breast cancer

- Green tea: 2-3 cups per day to prevent colorectal cancer, 4 cups per day to prevent cardiovascular disease, 4-5 cups per day to prevent systemic lupus, multiple sclerosis and rheumatoid arthritis.

- Kimchi: 1 1/5 cups per day to prevent hypertension

- Macadamia: 17 nuts per day to prevent colorectal cancer

- Mackerel: 1+ serving per week for macular degeneration, 3.5 oz. per day to prevent colorectal Cancer

- Mango: 2 fruits per day to prevent esophageal and head/neck cancer

- Nectarines: 2 fruits per day to prevent esophageal and head/neck cancer

- Olive oil: 3-4 tablespoons per day to prevent colorectal, laryngeal and breast cancer

- Oranges: 1.5 per day to prevent lupus

- Peaches: 2 fruits per day to prevent esophageal and head/neck cancer

- Pine nuts: ¼ cup per day to prevent colorectal cancer

- Plums: 2 fruits per day to prevent esophageal and head/neck cancer

- Purple potatoes: 5 small per day, to prevent colorectal cancer

- Red wine: 1/2 glass per day to prevent colorectal cancer; 1 glass per day to prevent atherosclerosis

- Salmon: 1+ servings per week to prevent macular degeneration, 3.5 oz. per day to prevent colorectal cancer

- Sardines: 1+ servings per week to prevent macular degeneration, 3.5 oz. per day to prevent colorectal cancer

- Soy milk: 1 cup per day to prevent breast cancer and atherosclerosis

- Strawberries: 1 ½ cups per day to prevent lupus

- Swordfish: 1+ servings per week to prevent macular degeneration, 3.5 oz. per day to prevent colorectal cancer

- Tuna: 1+ servings per week to prevent macular degeneration, 3.5 oz. per day to prevent colorectal cancer

- Walnut: 22 halves per day to decrease risk of colorectal cancer; 29 halves per week to reduce risk of death from stage 3 colorectal cancer

- Whole wheat: 2.7 servings per day to prevent cardiovascular disease and type 2 diabetes

- Yogurt less than 1 serving per day to prevent cardiovascular disease

Are you enjoying the book so far?

If so, please help us reach more readers by taking
30 seconds to write
just a few words on Amazon

**Thank you very much!
Now, let's continue...**

Background information about *Eat To Beat Disease*

The Amazon #1 bestseller in nutrition for cancer and Alzheimer's prevention, *Eat To Beat Disease* has been lauded by many readers. Arianna Huffington, Founder and CEO, Thrive Global calls Dr. William Li "a healthcare pioneer." She writes, "Dr. Li helps our readers thrive by unpacking how the body's own systems respond to what we eat. His book will give practical tips for healthier living and empower readers with ways they can help their bodies fight disease."

Super model Cindy Crawford enthuses, "Finally! A book that tells us the truth about what we can eat to be healthy, based on real science, from a true expert. *Eat to Beat Disease* will completely change the way you think about your body and the choices you make when you grocery shop, cook for your family, or dine out. Read this book from cover to cover if you want to be on top of your game for health, beauty, and fitness, from the inside out. When it comes to food and health, I'm so happy to have Dr. Li in my camp!"

The Washington Book Review calls the book a "ground-breaking study," and claims that, "Dr. William W. Li provides the knowledge and tools to make better decisions what to eat every day. This easy-to-read book is not a diet book but help you better understand what you eat."

Mark Hyman, MD, and the Director of the Cleveland Clinic Center praises the book, saying, "Unlike so many books that turn people away from the foods they enjoy, *Eat to Beat Disease* shows us how the foods we love actually support our wellbeing and vitality. I recommend that every health seeker read this new classic, and tell their friends and family all about it."

Nobel Laureate in Medicine Louis J. Ignarro has this to say about the book, "The time has come for 'health' to be properly defined and for us to understand clearly how food impacts health. *Eat to Beat Disease* delivers on this vision in a big way - and with real science to back it up. Dr. Li's highly enjoyable and informative book spreads the word that achieving great health is within reach for all of us, using the very foods that we love. *Eat to Beat Disease* will excite, amaze, and inspire us all to eat healthy and defeat disease. And remember - you are in control of your own destiny."

Background information about William W. Li, MD

Dr. William W. Li is a doctor specialized in internal medicine. He also has a career as a research scientist, based on his studies in biochemistry and biotechnology. For the last twenty-five years, he has also been the leader of the Angiogenesis Foundation, whose goal is to improve health around the globe.

How to Assess Your Risk

Answer the following questions and give yourself the assigned points. Keep track of the total points to find out your overall risk at the end of the questions.

1. Age: the older you are, the higher your risk for preventable chronic diseases.
   Under thirty = 0
   30-50 = +1
   Over 50 = +2

2. Body Mass Index: the higher your BMI, the higher your chances for certain diseases. You can calculate your BMI online with easy calculators, based on your weight and height.
   Normal BMI (18-25) = 0
   BMI 26-30 = +1
   BMI 30 = +2

3. Past Medical History: have you had any major diseases, including mental health conditions?
   Clean bill of health = 0
   One prior inactive disease = +1

More than one prior diseases or one active disease = +2

4. High risk factors: if you have any super high risk diseases, such as: keratosis, autoimmune diseases, alcoholic liver disease, barrett's esophagus, cardiovascular disease, endometriosis, hepatitis, HPV, hyperlipidemia, periodontitis, preeclampsia, renal insufficiency, traumatic head injury, or any type of diabetes, you are at an elevated risk.
Clean bill of health = 0
One high-risk disease = +1
More than one = +2

5. Family History: certain medical conditions in the family put you at an elevated risk, including: cancer-associated syndromes, Crohn's disease, high cholesterol, heritable cancers, neurodegenerative disease, any type of diabetes
Clean family bill of health = 0
Any heritable disease history = +2

6. Where you live
For cancer, the top ten states for risk in order are: Kentucky, Delaware, Louisiana, Pennsylvania, New York, Maine, New Jersey, Rhode Island and Connecticut. The worst countries are: Denmark, France, Australia, Belgium, Norway, Ireland, Korea, Netherlands and Caledonia.

For diabetes, the highest rates are found in: Puerto Rico, Guam, Mississippi, West Virginia, Kentucky, Alabama, Louisiana, Tennessee, Texas and Arkansas. Outside the US, the worst areas are: The Marshall Islands, Micronesia, Kiribati, French Polynesia, Saudi

Arabia, Vanuatu, Kuwait, Bahrain, Mauritius and New Caledonia.

For cardiovascular disease risk, the highest rates are found in: Kentucky, West Virginia, Louisiana, Oklahoma, Alabama, Mississippi, Michigan, Arkansas, Tennessee, and Texas.

Worldwide, the worst countries are: Russia, Ukraine, Romania, Hungary, Cuba, Brazil, Czech Republic, Argentina, and Mexico.
If you live in a top-ten risk area for one of these diseases = +1
If not = 0

7. Genetic risks: DNA tests can determine genetic risk.
If you have not had a DNA test or had no increased risk detected = 0
If you have a high risk for one disease = +1
If you have a high risk for two or more diseases = +2

8. Exposure to Toxic Chemicals: these common toxins pose an elevated risk:
Arsenic, asbestos, benzene, carbon tetrachloride, dioxin and DDT, formaldehyde, industrial dyes, lead, mercury, methylene chloride, paradichlorobenzene, perfluorinated chemicals, radiation, toluene, vape smoke, vinyl chloride.
If you have had no significant exposure = 0
If you have had one significant exposure = +1
If you have had more than one = +2

9. Tobacco Use
If you have never smoked = 0

If you were a previous smoker or lived or worked in proximity to smoke = +1

If you currently smoke or vape, or live or work in proximity to smoke = +2

10. Alcohol Use
If you don't drink at all = 0
If you drink modestly (one glass of red wine or beer per day, no liquor) = -1
More than one glass of red wine / beer or hard liquor = +1
Regularly drink hard liquor = +2

11. Extended Dietary Habits
Has your lifetime dietary pattern followed a Mediterranean or Asian diet (fresh ingredients, high in vegetables and dietary fiber?) = -1
Did you once have an unhealthy diet but now are eating healthily = 0
A western diet high in meat and light on veggies? = +1
Junk food diet? = +2

12. Exercise habits:
If you exercise regularly = -2
Occasional exercise = 0
No exercise = +2

13. Pet ownership:
If you own a pet now or in the past? = -1
No pet = 0

14. Did your mother breastfeed you?
Yes = -1
Uncertain = 0
No = +1

15. Night shift work
    Yes = +1
    No = 0

16. Stress Levels
    Low = 0
    Moderate = + 1
    High = +2

17. Age of parents' death from health problem:
    If both parents lived past fifty (or died of a non-illness related factor such as an accident)   = 0
    If one died of illness before fifty = +1
    If both died before fifty = +2

Scoring:

19-29 = Red zone / elevated risk

If you scored in this level, you have a very high risk of a major illness unless you make major lifestyle changes. You would definitely benefit from the 5x5x5 dietary plan.

10-18 = yellow zone / average risk

If you scored in this level, you are not in immediate danger, but you would do well to make some improvements in your lifestyle.

0-9 = green zone / lowest risk

If you scored in this level, that means you have the lowest possible risk of developing one of the major diseases. It means you are off to a great start in life, but remember that risk factors increase with age, so now is the time to incorporate healthy foods in your diet in order to keep yourself in this desirable category.

Thank You!

We hope you've enjoyed your reading experience. Our team at Summary Genie is constantly striving to deliver to you the highest quality summary guides. We'd like to thank you for supporting us and reading until the very end.

Before you go, would you kindly please leave us a review on Amazon? It would mean a lot to us and it will support our work in creating more high quality summary guides for you in the future.

Thank you once again!

Warmly yours,
The Summary Genie Team

Made in the USA
Coppell, TX
02 September 2021